Investment University's
Profit from China

Investment University's Profit from China

Investment U

BICENTENNIAL
1807
WILEY
2007
BICENTENNIAL

John Wiley & Sons, Inc.

Published by John Wiley & Sons, Inc., Hoboken, New Jersey.
Published simultaneously in Canada.

For general information on our other products and services or for technical support, please contact our Customer Care Department within the United States at (800) 762-2974, outside the United States at (317) 572-3993 or fax (317) 572-4002.

Wiley also publishes its books in a variety of electronic formats. Some content that appears in print may not be available in electronic books. For more information about Wiley products, visit our web site at www.wiley.com.

ISBN 0-470-12235-8

Printed in the United States of America.

10 9 8 7 6 5 4 3 2 1

Contents

This is our very own "dream team" of experts we turn to for guidance and gains. Frankly, they're the best at what they do: They generate more profits in any market than anyone else we know. And each of them fits the two key criteria that we demand of our experts:

1. They must each have a proven track record showing the ability to consistently pull profits from any market.

2. They must be able to communicate their strategies—no matter how complex—into simple ideas that our readers can easily apply to their own unique situations.

You should also know this about Investment U: Since it began in 1999, we've tried to deliver actionable investment wisdom to our readers each week.

Many of our strategies, techniques, or insights go against the prevailing conventional

b
h
ma

pen
how   done
in th   primarily through
our fr   ..rs, written in plain English and
using real-life examples, not textbook mumbo-jumbo.

The Investment University research team that has assembled this report consists of some of the most successful and profitable people in the industry, like Dr. Mark Skousen (Investment U chairman, former Columbia Economics professor and editor of *Forecasts & Strategies*), Alex Green (*Oxford Club* Investment Director and 16-year Wall Street veteran), Horacio Márquez . . . and a host of others.

wisdom. But at a time when most investment "how-to" books peddle stale ideas like "Buy and Hold" or "Dollar-Cost Averaging," we show you what really works today and how to make it work for you.

With that, I leave you to enjoy our report: Investment U's *Profit from China*. And I encourage you to visit our web site at www.investmentu.com/china to get our latest updates for the recommendations you're about to read.

I hope you enjoy learning how profitable investing really works.

Good Investing,

Julia Guth
Founder, Investment U

Introduction

China is unequivocally one of the hottest investments in today's market.

The country has transformed itself from an impoverished and closed agricultural society to a globally integrated industrial powerhouse. And investors who know how to position themselves now will make a lifetime of profits. . . .

In the past two years alone, stock funds in China have more than tripled the returns of the S&P 500. Its gross domestic product is growing at roughly 10 percent annually, compared to 3 percent or so in the United States. And consumer spending is growing at 13 percent.

The growth has enticed global businesses to quickly jump on board. Foreign direct investment totaled $51 billion last year, nearly double what it was in 1999. And it's projected to top $345 billion in the coming year.

The nation has lifted 400 million people out of poverty, a transition some call "the fastest change in human history." China's middle class, now estimated at 150 million to 200 million people, is expected to double in size in the next five years.

Today, Shanghai has 4,000 skyscrapers, twice the number in Manhattan, and plans to build an additional 2,000 in the next five years. And this is just one city in China. A very sustainable 9 to 10 percent annual GDP growth will make China a lucrative investment target for years to come.

The question is, of course, how do you safely invest in this unprecedented growth . . . and still walk away potentially doubling or tripling your money?

The problem of how to "play" this engine of productivity is amorphous and vague for all but the top investors like Warren Buffett, who has invested $1.2 billion in one of the recommendations in this report. After all, China is still a communist-run country, its government is unpredictable, financial reporting at public companies is less than transparent, and the country's stock market isn't liquid enough to safely invest in. But there are profitable alternatives. . . .

We prefer to invest in foreign companies China relies on to fuel its economy and support its 1.3 billion people. It's an indirect, safer way to make money from China's massive appetite for growth.

Investors who get into these investments now stand a great likelihood of seeing very healthy gains in the coming weeks, months, and years, many of which will be commodity driven like the ones below:

- China's demand for steel caused the prices to double . . . and investors made 553 percent on Mittal Steel Company in 13 months. . . .

- China's demand for copper pushed Phelps-Dodge, the world's largest miner, up 253 percent in 16 months.

- China's unquenchable thirst for oil drained supply from OPEC and pushed prices up by 63 percent. Investors in Valero Energy, the nation's largest refinery, collected 431 percent in 24 months.

- China's demand for concrete pushed prices up and investors in Cemex S.A., one of the largest concrete suppliers in the world, made 143 percent in 21 months.

The advice and recommendations in this report come from a dedicated group of investment professionals who have visited China, studied the culture, and identified specifically what makes its economy tick . . . and will keep your portfolio ticking for years to come.

We invite you to study this book carefully. . . . It profiles some of the key companies Investment U has identified to take advantage of the burgeoning markets in commodities, resources, and even banking. And the potential returns are tremendous.

To be sure, China represents the fastest-growing investment opportunity we've seen in more than 35 years. And you now have early access to the safest, most rewarding ways to profit.

P.S. We've built an exclusive web site dedicated to updating the recommendations that follow. Only those who have purchased this report will have access. I urge you to visit http://www .investmentu.com/china to get the latest pricings and material information regarding these specific investment opportunities.

Our 12 Timeless Rules of Investing

1. **An attempt at making a quick buck often leads to losing much of that buck.** The people who suffer the worst losses are those who over-reach. If the investment sounds too good to be true, it is. The best hot tip we've found is "there is no such thing as a hot tip."

2. **Don't let a small loss become large.** Don't keep losing money just to "prove you are right." Never throw good money after bad (don't buy more of a loser). When all you're left with is hope, get out.

3. **Cut your losers; let your winners ride.** Avoid limited-upside, unlimited-downside investments. Don't fall in love with your investment; it won't fall in love with you.

4. **A rising tide raises all ships, and vice versa. So assess the tide, not the ships.** Fighting the prevailing "trend" is generally a recipe for disaster. Stocks will fall more than you think and rise higher than you can imagine. In the short run, values don't matter.

5. **When a stock hits a new high, it's not time to sell . . . something is going right.** When a stock hits a new low, it's not time to buy, something is wrong.

6. **Buy and hold doesn't ALWAYS work.** If stocks don't seem cheap, stand aside.

7. **Bear markets begin in good times. Bull markets begin in bad times.**

8. **If you don't understand the investment, don't buy it.** Don't be wooed. Either make an effort to understand it or say "no thanks." You can't know everything, so don't stray far from what you know.

9. **Buy value, and sell hysteria.** Paying less than the underlying asset's value is a proven successful strategy. Buying overvalued stocks has proven to underperform

the market. Neglected sectors often offer good values. The "popular" sectors are often overvalued.

10. **Investing in what's popular never ends up making you any money.** Avoid popular stocks, fad industries, and new ventures. Buy an investment when it has few friends.

11. **When it's time to act, don't hesitate.** Once you're in, be patient and don't be rattled by fluctuations. Stick with your plan . . . but when you make a mistake, don't hesitate. Learn more from your bad moves than your good ones.

12. **Expert investors care about risk; novice investors shop for returns.** If you focus on the risks, the returns will eventually come for you. If you focus on the returns, the risks will eventually come for you.

To receive many more of these investment truths and much more, sign up to receive the FREE, twice weekly *Investment U E-Letter.* Just visit: http://www.investmentu.com.

Investment University's Profit from China

The "Waking Giant" of the Twenty-First Century Is Set to Power the World's Economy . . . and Investor Returns

The nineteenth century belonged to Britain. The twentieth century belonged to the United States. And the twenty-first century will belong to China.

—Jim Rogers, co-founder of the Quantum Fund

Despite its communist history, for more than a decade China has been a free-market economy, taking the first steps from being a Third World economy to being a global economic powerhouse. When controls are loosened and business is encouraged by the government of an emerging economy—even a communist one—the results can be astonishing.

Hundreds of inefficient state-run enterprises are being privatized. That means there are more than 1.3 billion people who are free to become entrepreneurs in a country set to become the biggest economic force the world has ever known.

As the *Wall Street Journal* noted, China has already become "the world's factory floor." If you doubt this claim, consider that today China makes . . .

- More than 50 percent of the world's cameras;
- More than 35 percent of the televisions sold worldwide;
- More than 30 percent of the air conditioners sold worldwide;
- More than 25 percent of the washing machines sold worldwide;
- More than 22 percent of the refrigerators sold worldwide;

And . . .

- General Electric expects purchases from China to hit $5 billion annually for the next three years.
- A single private Chinese company now accounts for 40 percent of all the microwave ovens sold in Europe each year.
- The city of Wenzhou, in eastern China, sells 70 percent of the world's metal cigarette lighters.
- China's economy has been growing at a rate three times greater than that of the United States.

And, as you'll learn, that's just the tip of the iceberg. Economic growth has brought with it greater individual freedom for the Chinese. Even restrictions on religion and family life are relaxing.

Despite the government's communist rhetoric, China's people are steadily ensuring the American dream becomes the Chinese dream. Unlike the past, millions of Chinese today are living like those in the West—consuming more meat, driving more cars, traveling the globe, and otherwise spending their rapidly expanding incomes, in much the same way Americans do.

Let's take a look at what's behind all this growth.

The Driving Force behind China's Growth

There's a combination of unique factors contributing to the country's investment potential:

- A massive population, starting from a low wealth base;
- A work ethic second to none;
- A sense of social stability;
- A strong commitment to education;
- A high savings rate of over 30 percent; and
- A powerful desire to succeed and become wealthy.

China is easily the world's fastest-growing major economy and is creating billions of dollars in new wealth. Imagine how your own business would perform if the U.S. economy were growing at 9 percent a year.

Although there are many stocks that will benefit from this explosive growth, one sector in particular is going to profit from the needs of China's burgeoning population.

Think Commodities, Think China

The Earth Policy Institute reports that China has already eclipsed the United States as the world's #1 consumer of overall raw material and growth-related commodities like grain, coal, and steel. And, its consumption of raw materials, as a percentage of world totals, doubles each decade. Consider this:

- China spurred 40 percent of global oil demand growth since 2000.
- Despite China's one-child policy, the population keeps growing, as does the demand for basic food commodities. And supply is increasingly tight. The per-capita consumption of soybeans in China has grown an average of 4 percent each year since 1994, and vegetable oil consumption has grown at twice that rate.
- The Chinese market for steel has averaged 20 percent annual increases since 2000 and is expected to rise for at least the next three years. As Chinese skyscrapers, bridges, and other infrastructure swiftly materialize, seemingly out of thin air, demand for steel increases.
- The International Energy Agency predicts the world will have to spend an average of $550 billion to keep up with the electricity demand every year . . . for the next 25 years. China and India are look-

ing to be at the forefront of energy demand. In China, the booming economy has boosted electricity demand 150 percent over the past 20 years.

In the past five years, U.S. exports to China have more than doubled to $35 billion, while exports to other areas of the world have only grown by 2 percent.

And yet most investors have virtually no money invested in this region. It may sound counter-intuitive, but this is actually an excellent sign because, as we'll demonstrate, many more investors will soon be clamoring for a piece of the action.

The Uptrend in Commodities Is Global, but China Is the Driving Force

In the late 1990s, commodities were in a long-running slump of almost 25 years. If you had walked into Merrill Lynch, the nation's largest brokerage house, they would have politely told you they didn't handle commodities any more.

And that's unfortunate. Since January 1999, silver prices are up 40 percent. Gold's rocketed 53 percent. Steel prices have more than doubled. Uranium's exploded 180 percent, and oil prices jumped a blistering 500 percent.

So what's going on?

For an answer to that question, we spoke to Jim Rogers, one of the best investors of all time and someone who has made a career (and millions of dollars) by visiting and investing in foreign countries. He knows that the secret to making real money through global investing is to buy stocks when nobody wants them.

According to Rogers, we're "in the beginning of a multiyear bull market in commodities." In fact, it's likely to last at least another 10 years. Commodity prices have been too cheap for too long. And now we're in the "catch-up" phase of this bull market.

In our interview with Rogers, he made it clear that he expects commodities to beat all other investments for the next 10 years. The world's top

---

The Man Who Made 40 Times His Money in a Decade. In 2003, Jim Rogers wrote about a new bull market in commodities that could last a very long time . . . and that it was just getting underway. He said that nobody was paying attention.

Three years later, he couldn't have been more right. Now people are paying attention and asking, "When will the commodity bull market end?

Read our most recent interview with Jim in **Investment U E-Letter** issue number 543. There, you'll find out why he thinks the Fed will fail, what's in store for emerging markets (including the only one he's currently investing in), and life's most important lessons. To access, go to www .investmentu.com.

commodity guru took time to share specific plays for taking full advantage of this historic opportunity:

IU: Do you anticipate a major consolidation in commodities?

JR: Yes, I do. Something's going to cause consolidations in commodities. We always have consolidations in every bull market in history, no matter what the asset class. In every stock bull market, there have been consolidations along the way.

Again, I wish I were smart enough to tell you exactly what's going to cause them, and the timing, but I'm not. It's pretty obvious to me that if we suddenly see headlines in the *Wall Street Journal* of some kind of turmoil in China, that commodities would be having a correction, or would go into a correction. But that would be a chance to BUY commodities.

You know, in the 1980s and 1990s, we had some huge corrections in stocks. In 1987, stocks went down what, 35 to 40 percent in several months, but people who understood that this was in the context of a major bull market bought more stocks; they didn't panic and sell.

Likewise, in 1994 or any of the other corrections along the way in the bull market in stocks in the 1980s and 1990s, you made a lot of money. So if you see those headlines, I urge you to buy all the commodities you can. Probably buy all the China you can, too; but certainly, buy all the commodities you can.

IU: So if China slows down or crashes that would be a tremendous buying opportunity in China and commodities?

JR: In terms of commodities, yes . . . especially in terms of commodities, but also in terms of China.

If we suddenly have a bird-flu epidemic throughout Europe, I suspect economies around the world will decline and scare people and commodities will slow down for a while. If Fannie Mae goes bankrupt, it's going to scare people. If China goes to war with Taiwan, it's going to scare people.

Something's going to cause consolidations, but buy 'em, don't sell 'em.

IU: If you were going to go into one raw commodity, what would it be?

JR: I'd go into probably one of the agricultural commodities, if I could only go into one right now, because most of them are still very, very depressed, and that's where I think you would find better opportunities.

You can look at lots of things. In the 1970s, world economies were in the tank, but we had a big bull market in commodities because there was no supply. So even though demand slowed down, supply went down even faster, so you had this gigantic bull market.

It's one of the things that's happening in oil right now: Supply is going down. You know, if you find a huge oil field in Berlin or Tokyo or somewhere, it'll have an effect. But supplies are going down in all this stuff. And that's why I'm so optimistic on commodities.

IU: Are you moving your offices from New York to Shanghai?

JR: Well, that's one reason we're here, because we're contemplating moving to a Chinese-speaking city, and Shanghai is at the top of the list—at the moment, anyway.

We have a 25-month-old baby girl, and she's bilingual. We got her a Chinese nanny from the beginning, whose instructions were to only speak Mandarin to the baby. So she is literally bilingual, at age 25 months, and we're doing everything we can to encourage and develop that.

There are a lot of exciting things going on in China and in Chinese-speaking areas. They're letting Chinese institutions invest abroad now. Chinese tourists can get passports easily now. . . . And they can take, I think, up to $6,000 if they go on a trip. So you're starting to see huge amounts of Chinese travel.

And, they're taking steps toward making [the yuan] a completely convertible currency. It will happen by 2007, under the terms of the World Trade contract they have—you know, they joined the World Trade Organization. And they've got the Olympics in 2008. So certainly by 2008, they're not going to be sitting around here with a blocked currency anymore . . . [in the] longer term, the yuan's going to be a big currency, a great currency.

The way we see it, when one of America's top investors decides to raise his daughter to speak Chinese, you know he's serious about the future of the country. For the full interview with Jim Rogers, visit www.investmentu.com.

Why China, Why Now?

In short, China's domestic economy has become a powerful engine of growth, and it's not going to stop anytime soon. And as global investors, we want to capitalize on it. But we're not simply seeking to make big profits. We're out to make a killing.

The *Fortune* 500 companies are already falling over themselves to take advantage of what's happening in the world's most populous nation. For instance:

- Microsoft says that it intends to invest $750 million in China over the next three years.
- Ford plans to boost its purchases of auto parts in China to as much as $1 billion annually.
- General Electric expects purchases from China—both parts and finished goods—to hit $5 billion annually in the next three years.
- Wal-Mart concedes that more than $10 billion in Chinese-made goods are sold in its stores every year.
- Motorola says its total investment in China will hit a record $50 billion this year.

As you can see, the biggest and most savvy investors in the United States—the *Fortune* 500—are already putting money to work in this rapidly growing region at breakneck speed. Unlike the average investor, they are fully aware of the historic opportunity here.

But please don't think we're suggesting you can throw darts in this part of the world and make money. That's not the case at all. There's no getting round it, China can be a treacherous place to invest for those who don't have special, intimate knowledge of what's going on. Fortunes have been lost investing in emerging markets over the past 10 years. And China is no exception.

The Safest Way to Invest in a Risky Part of the World. The stock exchange in Shanghai is wild and unregulated. Disclosure is limited. In truth, China's exchanges aren't so much efficient capital markets as giant casinos.

Most of China's public companies trade on either the Shanghai or Shenzhen stock exchanges. There are two classes of stock: A-shares, which are denominated in yuan and, until recently, could only be owned by Chinese citizens; and B-shares, which are denominated in dollars and can be bought by foreigners.

You'll want to pass on both, trust us. (B-shares, in particular, are mostly failed privatizations, the sorriest bunch of public companies on the far side of the Pacific.)

It's best to focus your efforts on companies that are big enough, sound enough—and honest enough—to list their shares on the New York Stock Exchange. The reasons are straightforward:

- The liquidity is better.
- The spreads are smaller.
- The commissions are lower.
- Most importantly, these companies use Western accounting practices—and publish their annual and quarterly reports in English.

So, we need to turn our eyes homeward and carefully pick those investments that are going to multiply—no matter what.

It is also important to note that we're not talking about a single stock, set to revolutionize the markets. It's about profiting from history in the making . . . a colossal shift in global economies . . . unlike anything investors have ever seen.

That's why the *Fortune* 500 makes direct investments rather than buying a stake in companies listed on the Shanghai stock exchange.

And you shouldn't be risking your hard-earned capital on the Chinese exchange either. That's much too risky. You want to stack the deck in your favor instead. That means targeting high-return, low-risk opportunities in this part of the world.

The Bull Hunter Zeroes in on China

While compiling this report, we spoke with Dan Denning, author of *The Bull Hunter*, a *New York Times* best seller about unearthing opportunities destined to provide ground-floor investors with safe, outsized profit opportunities in countries, industries, and sectors that are at the beginning of huge bull markets.

During a visit to China, Dan had some interesting insights into these emerging markets. His take is that China is the story that matters most if you're asking what the world will look like the day after reckoning day.

In the short term, you've got a bank system loaded down with bad debts and overinvestment in commercial real estate. But you've also got a country consuming half the world's cement, with a voracious demand for iron ore and other raw materials.

That demand might slow down because of government intervention (through higher interest rates to contain inflation). Or it might go through normal free-market booms and busts.

One thing's for sure: it's not anywhere close to letting up.

But some economists have begun to complain that China is actually growing too fast and investing too much. The chief concern is that the Chinese have over invested in fixed capital. Credit excesses in the United States lead to rising asset prices and consumption. In China, they lead, so the theory goes, to reckless bank lending and overproduction of manufactured goods.

Is China Building Too Many Factories?

Before we try to decide whether having too many factories producing too much stuff is really a problem (or a worse problem than not having enough factories at all), let's look at the numbers.

China's gross fixed investment spending is equal to about 46 percent of its GDP as of 2004 (latest available). That's a high percentage. According to the CIA *World Factbook*, it's the fourth-highest percentage of 146 nations surveyed. (The United States comes in at 127th, with about 15 percent of GDP going to fixed capital investment.)

But is it too much? Or, in economic terms, can a government efficiently and productively manage the task of investing $700 billion a year in fixed capital projects? Or is it inevitably going to lead to bubbles and overinvestment in certain sectors?

Again going to the data, we see that 25 percent of China's investment in fixed assets is in manufacturing. No surprise there. But that does not, de facto, constitute a bubble.

China's National Bureau of Statistics lists 30 separate categories of fixed-asset investments in manufacturing. No single manufacturing category accounts for more than 3.5 percent of total fixed investment (ferrous metal smelting commands the largest percentage, at 3.5 percent).

If you look at the growth rates of investment in particular sectors, you get an idea of where China's planners think China's needs lie. Investment in ferrous metal mining grew 256 percent in the first eight months of this year compared to last. Oil processing, coking plants, and nuclear material processing grew by 127.5 percent. Wood processing investment grew by 71 percent; furniture, manufacturing investment rose 52 percent, and general metal products investment jumped 57.4 percent.

China, it appears, is trying to turn itself into a steel superpower. When you see the internal growth projects later, you'll see why. But the important point now is that these are the investment priorities of an industrializing nation.

There's really nothing shocking about any of the numbers you see here. In fact, the deeper you dig, the more you'll see signs that China is using its $54 billion in annual foreign direct investment deliberately and pragmatically. It's building itself an industrial base on the back of

Western capital. Not bad for a nation that didn't have a lot of capital to begin with.

Investment in transportation was 11.5 percent of all fixed-asset spending. Road construction made up 7.6 percent of all investment. New water projects, such as the Three Gorges Dam, made up 8.2 percent. These are simple needs for a massive country.

And, don't forget: more water, more energy, more roads, more iron, and more steel. The Chinese are importing factories, roads, dams, and the entire industrial infrastructure of a developed economy.

On top of that, China's domestic consumption is rising just as quickly. After all, the Chinese want to live the good life, too, not just provide it to Americans at a discount. Savings rates are high in China. But there are major trends powering domestic consumption. A whole new nation-in-waiting is poised to move out of low-paying agricultural jobs in the hinterlands into higher-wage jobs in China's urban centers.

But as living standards rise in China, it suddenly becomes an investment market in its own right, a place where you want to sell your company's products, not just have them made there. It will take years for average living standards in China to rise to Western levels, if, in fact, that's even possible in a nation of more than a billion people. But even if GDP per capita in China lags behind the West for years, there will still be immense GDP growth fueled by domestic demand.

In any event, there will be booms and busts in Chinese stocks. But for truly long-term investors, anything that profits from the development of Chinese infrastructure, financial services, and health services is the best way to profit from development inside China.

Risks to the Dragon's Serene Future

China faces an enormous test, the likes of which has not been seen before: how to manage the transition of hundreds of millions of people from subsistence-level, labor-intensive farming, to labor-intensive manufacturing done in cities of 15 million people.

It's a mass migration no government could possibly manage. One way or another, the market will have to manage it. But the free market is not a school-crossing officer or social worker. It does not wait to make sure every last person keeps up.

Growing quickly when you're enormous to begin with is not without very real risks. Investors who think making money in Chinese stocks will be an easy matter are mistaken. Everyone knows the story of China's miracle growth. But if you spend a few hours in any major Chinese city, you'll see that growth has had some unintended consequences.

For example, there are now more than 160 days a year when visibility in Hong Kong due to pollution is less than five miles. The culprits are factories in Shenzhen.

But don't expect poor air quality to slow down Chinese demand for raw materials. There are large appetites in China. Less than 100 years after the end of the feudal system, and less than 30 years after the communists opened up to the West again, China is clearly open for business. It has huge needs. Who will meet them? How can you profit?

Part II

How Enormous Fortunes Will Be Made behind the Great Wall

The numbers we've talked about allow you to see the vast impact China is already having on the world economy. Yet, China's race for worldwide economic domination is far from over.

You see, China's entry into the World Trade Organization (WTO) at the end of 2001 is accelerating all these positive economic trends at warp speed. WTO membership is giving China tremendous advantages. It cuts production costs, forces down tariffs, and removes obstacles to selling overseas.

That, in turn, is drawing record direct investment to China. In fact, more than $600 billion has been invested over the past two decades.

According to the Goldman Sachs, one of the world's leading investment banking firms:
As today's advanced economies become a shrinking part of the world economy, the accompanying shifts in spending could provide significant opportunities for global companies. Being invested in and involved in the right markets—particularly the right emerging markets— may become an increasingly important strategic choice. (Goldman Sachs, "Global Economics Paper No: 99: Dreaming with BRICs: The Path to 2050," 2003)

Some people call it globalization. We think of it as the "money migration." Simply, it means that money (capital) will always migrate to where the returns are highest. When it migrates, it brings investment, jobs, new incomes, and prosperity with it. Today, money is migrating from West to East. If jobs are moving East because there are more new projects—driven by cheap labor—that promise higher returns on investment, where should you invest? What are the investment consequences of the money migration?

The answer is simple: When money like that continues to pour into a market, prices tend to go up, especially for companies best poised to ride the massive influx of capital.

We've selected four China plays that will benefit from the upcoming surge in economic growth. From oil and seeds, to an Exchange

Traded Fund (ETF) offering 25 diverse slices of China in one investment, to the bank with the strongest foothold in China, these positions are primed for profit.

Opportunity 1: Crude Awakening: How to Profit from China's Growing Oil Addiction

Today, the entire world faces an unprecedented problem. Like it or not, the key resource on which we have built our global economy—cheap energy—is running out. And shrinking energy resources equal soaring energy prices.

It's a simple case of supply and demand.

It took 125 years to consume the first trillion barrels of oil. Now it's estimated we'll use the next trillion in less than 30 years. Of course, China will be among the leading consumers as it continues to fuel massive growth that, by 2050, could make China the world's largest economy—and the largest energy consumer.

However, this is also creating an unprecedented investment opportunity. It's one that offers a low-risk way to capitalize on the torrid expansion of the world's fastest-growing major economy: **PetroChina** (NYSE: PTR).

PetroChina Is a Huge, Looming Giant

This is a pure play on China's ravenous thirst for energy. And it is perfectly positioned to make investors a good deal of money as China's economy expands. Let's start with two unassailable facts:

1. China has developed a world-class hydrocarbon addiction.
2. PetroChina is Asia's most profitable oil and gas company.

In April 2005, Hong Kong's FinanceAsia—the largest Asian-based financial publishing company—judged PetroChina as the region's "best oil and gas company," and the "best managed company."

Here are just a few of the ways PetroChina makes money:

- Exploration, development, and production of crude oil and natural gas;
- Refining, transportation, storage, import, and export of crude oil and petroleum products;
- Production and sale of chemical products; and
- Transmission, marketing, and sale of natural gas.

Last year, the company reported net income of $13.3 billion on revenue of $48 billion. Operating margins now top 37 percent. And management is earning a prodigious 28 percent return on equity.

If you lined up the amount of oil American residents use each day in one-gallon cans, you could encircle the earth almost six times.

The reason isn't hard to discern. . . .

China: The Number 1 Consumer of Raw Material and Growth-Related Commodities

According to the International Energy Agency, the average global demand for oil is over 88 million barrels a day. We use 200 tons of oil per second.

America only has 29 billion barrels of oil reserves left, enough to meet demand for two years. Meanwhile, China and India hunger for vast amounts of energy to satisfy a combined population of 2.3 billion people who are demanding the comforts of a growing industrial economy.

According to the Earth Policy Institute, China has already eclipsed the United States as the world's #1 consumer of overall raw material and growth-related commodities. Oil consumption by China, which stands at 6.5 million barrels a day, has jumped faster than many predictions. The nation is now expected to use 14 million barrels a day by 2025.

But while oil use in the United States increased by only 15 percent in the past decade, China's use of oil more than doubled in that period. Having recently overtaken Japan as an oil consumer, China is now second only to the United States:

- China currently imports 32 percent of its oil and is expected to double its need for imported oil between now and 2010.
- China spurred 40 percent of global oil demand growth since 2000.
- China increased its oil stockpiles 25 percent in the last calendar year.
- Demand is expected to grow by 7.4 percent this year, on top of last year's blistering 16 percent growth.

Automobiles are a symbol of aspiration, and the number of cars on Chinese mainland roads—already more than 20 million—is expected to increase by 2.5 million this year alone. That's a lot of tanks that'll need filling.

Is "Peak Oil" Already upon Us?

Supplies of oil, on the other hand, have started a permanent downward spiral, dwindling daily, made worse by the fact, up until recently, that there hadn't been a readily available major new oil field discovery in more than 20 years. And even the recent discovery won't be enough to make a dramatic change in that trend.

Be very clear: An energy crisis to dwarf the two previous ones in the 1970s isn't on the way. It is here already.

A Saudi spokesman told the *Financial Times* recently that if demand continues to grow at current rates, it will become "extremely difficult" for producers to pump enough oil to meet demand over the next 10 or 15 years. That's coming from one of the most oil-rich countries in the world.

From bottlenecks caused by aging refineries and supertanker shortage, to declining production from non-OPEC producers, the price of crude is being pushed up because of one simple fact: There isn't enough of it:

- In 2004, the oil industry was buzzing with news that the biggest deposit found in the last 10 years was discovered in the North Sea. Put into perspective, this new field will supply global oil requirements for just over five days.
- Earlier in 2006, a group led by Chevron discovered what some call the biggest domestic oil find in 38 years off the coasts of Louisiana and Texas. It could expand the U.S. reserves by 50 percent. However, the first drop of oil from this Gulf of Mexico find isn't expected to hit the market until at least 2010, and at best it will

only slow the decline in annual U.S. production.

- Some 90 percent of oil being extracted from the earth today is from oil fields that were discovered some 20 years ago, and new discoveries are both rare and insignificant.

China's unquenchable thirst for energy has played a major role in pushing up oil prices worldwide. See Figure 2.1.

If You Think $70 Oil Is Expensive, Read On . . .

While oil prices have fluctuated in 2006, they did hit an all-time high of $70 a barrel. Realistically, oil won't disappear overnight, but the days of cheap oil are over.

Some claim the fallout from the war in Iraq and unrest in the Middle East has spooked the markets. The thing is, what is the likelihood of a decline in terrorism? When might terrorists become less inclined to blow up a pipeline?

Matthew Simmons, an energy investment banker and advisor to the Bush administration says: "We need to price oil realistically to control its demand. That is because global production is peaking."

Why You Should Invest in Asia's Most Profitable Oil Company

Global production is peaking just as China's demand is beginning to soar—and that's setting up a profit play of historic proportions for PetroChina shareholders.

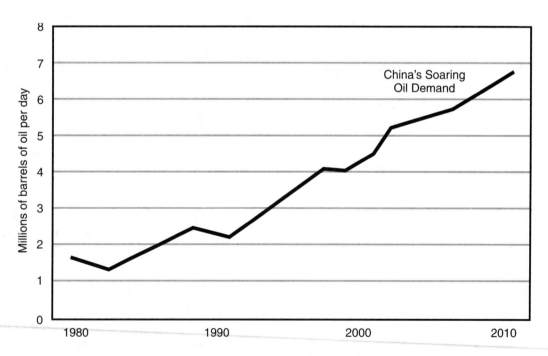

Figure 2.1   China's Demand for Oil Increasing by the Day

Consider that the company has 17,400 gasoline stations in China. It controls more than 29 percent of retail gasoline sales. And its pipelines stretch across more than 2,500 miles of the People's Republic.

So how did PetroChina get so big, with tentacles spanning China?

The oil giant is a former state-owned company that has been partially privatized. (The state retains a 90 percent stake.) In this case, partial privatization isn't so much a negative as a positive. The Chinese government has not only assigned it the country's choice oil fields, but also its best gas reserves.

A Buffett Connection . . . and 840 Billion Cubic Feet of Profit Potential

All told, PetroChina has 10.8 billion barrels of oil equivalent in reserves. (And its natural gas output climbed 21 percent last year to 840 billion cubic feet.)

The company is also expanding its reserves outside the country. Already PetroChina has major projects in Indonesia and Kazakhstan.

Despite this company's prodigious earnings growth—and future prospects—the stock is reasonably priced. A popular rule of thumb in picking stocks is to consider a stock underpriced if its PEG ratio (price to growth) falls much below 1. The PEG ratio (five year expected) for PetroChina is 0.25.

Need further assurance? You might note that Warren Buffett holds a $1.2 billion stake in PetroChina, through Berkshire Hathaway. The world's greatest investor never invests without a margin of safety.

And if it's good enough for Warren . . .

In short, we believe PetroChina is the ultimate play on China's booming energy consumption.

What about the risks involved? There are some, to be sure. The Communist Party remains an obstacle to the unfettered development of the private sector. The country has major social problems, and state banks hold mountains of bad debt. We think the enormous upside potential here makes taking this risk worthwhile.

Action to Take

Buy **PetroChina** (NYSE: PTR) at market. And use a 25 percent trailing stop to protect your principal and your profits. (See pages 26–28 for trailing stop information.) Please note: Visit www.investmentu.com/china for important updates regarding this specific recommendation.

Opportunity 2: The Single Best Stock to Feed China's Ravenous Appetite

When you're looking at the Asian story as an investor, it's easy to get lost in the big ideas. There are a lot of them. Has Japan turned the corner? What will happen to commodity prices now that 4 billion more people are competing for the same scarce natural resources? Where are the good businesses at good values?

The answer is pretty simple really: You ask yourself the same questions when buying stocks in Asia that you'd ask yourself in America. How does the company make money? How does it make more money than that? How much do you have to pay for this year's earnings? Does the business make sense to you?

Smart investors will make money finding little-known technology and manufacturing companies in Asia. Those stories are sexier. The potential payouts are enormous. So are the risks and earnings multiples.

We prefer to focus on businesses satisfying a known demand with a profitable product.

A Company That Feeds the World—And Makes a Profit Doing It

That's why we recommend buying Bunge (NYSE: BG) right now. Bunge is engaged in an easy-to-understand business: It helps feed the world and makes a profit doing it.

Bunge is a global agribusiness and food company with integrated operations that stretch from the farm field to the retail shelf and circle the globe. It has its hand in:

- Producing and selling fertilizer to farmers.
- Buying, handling, and selling oilseeds and grains.
- Crushing oilseeds to make meal and oil for the livestock and food-processing industries.
- Producing edible oils and related products for food-service customers and consumers.

By buying shares of Bunge, we are counting on three forces being in our favor—and staying that way:

1. Commodities being in a long-term (secular) bull market that supports food prices.
2. The fundamental shift in global economic fortunes from the West to the East (the money migration).
3. The debt-burdened U.S. dollar leading to an inevitable global currency realignment: the world getting off the dollar standard, and Asian central banks dumping their trillions' worth of dollar assets.

Forget Minor Fluctuations: The Overall Trend Is Up

Each of these three forces suggests a powerful driver behind higher prices for certain stocks, Bunge included. It won't be a straight line up to overnight profits. In fact, China and all of Asia are entering a cycle of mini booms and mini busts. The important fact to note is that the overall trend is up.

Asia today is similar to the United States in the nineteenth century. It's a volatile place with a wildcat mentality. Back then, all of North America was industrializing, modernizing, and fantasizing about a richer future. Now it's Asia's turn.

Fortunes will be made. Thousands of new businesses will be created. It's happening in China as we speak. But regardless of the business, the fundamental economic demands of human beings are not going to change, and that in itself is the basis of a powerful and relatively safe investment idea: Invest in the businesses that directly feed the growing trends.

So what does all this have to do with Bunge? Quite a lot.

Despite smaller populations in Europe and Japan, world population is growing. That means more people are competing for the same scarce resources. And when it comes to food, those resources are already stretched thin.

The U.S. Department of Agriculture publishes a report called "World Agricultural Supply and Demand Estimates" (WASDE). Here are some issue highlights:

- **Price pressures build:** Wheat stocks, the surplus amount of wheat in storage, are actually at 30-year lows. The report says price pressures will soon start building because wheat stockpiles have not been dramatically built.

- **Grain consumption exceeds production:** In all of the last four years, world grain production has fallen short of consumption, forcing a drawdown of stocks in wheat, corn, rice, and soybeans. Soybean prices recently hit 15-year highs, and wheat and corn seven-year highs.

- **Reserves being drawn down:** Despite the projection of the largest U.S. corn crop in history, the WASDE report said that the global stocks-to-use ratio for corn will be at a 30-year low, with stocks drawing down for the fifth straight year.

These numbers aren't actually bad news; quite the contrary. We don't believe we're headed for a Malthusian famine. What these statistics show us, coupled with what is on the ground everywhere in Asia is that there is a tremendous opportunity for food growers.

Profiting from a "Bedrock Economic Truth of Our Lifetime"

Long term, based on the population statistics, the demand for basic food commodities is one of the bedrock economic truths of our lifetimes. Food is in growing demand, and supply is increasingly tight. You don't have to be

an economist to understand a story like this. And you don't even have to be from a big family, where opening your mouth to speak at the dinner table means you have less time to shove in mashed potatoes before they disappear.

The argument for food (and for a select few other raw commodity companies) is basic common sense. It's an investment theme that's easy to understand and hard to argue with. And not only are the numbers behind you on this trend, but the returns on your investment over the next five years will be as good as anything else you can get in the world.

Bunge Is Filling Global Bellies—Fast

Don't be surprised if you haven't heard that China is tightening rules on soybean oil imports. It's not exactly making headlines. But that's okay. It means very few investors are looking at the investment opportunity in food, agriculture, and raw materials.

There's an old saying in China that the Chinese will eat anything under the sky with four legs, except the table and chair. And you wouldn't have to go far from a Chinese dinner table—or any dinner table in Asia for that matter—to see the moneymaking opportunity that Asia's gaping appetite provides. If you knew what you were looking for, that is.

What you're looking for is cooking oil—soybean oil, especially. Cooking oil is used in woks all over China—and all over the world, for that matter. Soybeans are key to the food product. China used to be the largest soybean *producer* and is now the largest soybean *importer*.

The Modern Food-Oil Connection. From farm to plate, the modern food system relies heavily on cheap oil. Threats to our oil supply also threaten our food supply.

China is way ahead of the United States in grain consumption and is expected to hit a record 500 tons in 2005 to 2006. The world's fastest-growing economy consumes more wheat and rice than any other country, and comes second to the United States only in corn usage.

As food undergoes more processing and travels farther, the food system consumes ever more energy each year. As oil supplies fluctuate, prices of foodstuffs can soar overnight.

Crop production now relies on fertilizers to replace soil nutrients, and therefore on the oil needed to mine, manufacture, and transport these fertilizers around the world.

World fertilizer use has increased dramatically since the 1950s. China is expected to use 56 million tons in 2006, up from 41 million tons just two years ago. Fertilizer use has leveled off in the United States, staying near 19 million tons per year since 1984.

Bunge is set to profit from both the oil and food shortages, which can only mean good things for investors.

Compete Globally, Feed Locally

Chinese soybean dependency is getting so large, in fact, that the government has raised requirements on soybean import quality in a bid to favor the domestic industry. By the way, this is just one part of what we see as an overall strategy by China to build institutions that make China less dependent on foreign commodities in financial markets.

Where you see it most is in the sprouting up of commodity exchanges in Dalian (North Korea), Zhenzhou, and Shanghai. The Chinese are trying to provide domestic producers with cheaper ways to sell production forward and hedge future price risk. It's all an attempt to make sure Chinese agriculture and industry can compete globally and feed locally.

With soybean prices at 15-year highs and Chinese demand at record levels, it's easy to see why the government is concerned. It's also easy to see why soybeans and soybean oil are a great China investment opportunity.

Bunge is in a perfect position to profit from China's strategy of securing flows of raw materials from neutral countries around the world. Here's why.

Bunge—A Truly Global Company with a Strong Presence in China

Bunge is the world's largest oilseed processing company. It's the largest producer and supplier of fertilizers to farmers in South America. And it's the world's leading seller of bottled vegetable oil to consumers. From raw materials to finished product, Bunge has a strong position in its market.

In Argentina, Bunge is the country's largest soy processor. It's also the largest wheat producer and fertilizer manufacturer in the country. It's the second-largest agricultural exporter in the country and the third-largest exporter, period.

What's Bunge's connection with the Chinese market, you're wondering?

The company doesn't make its export market numbers available on a line-item basis. It does point out, however, that per capita consumption of soybeans in China has grown at 4 percent a year since 1994, and that vegetable oil consumption has grown at twice that rate.

Bunge is an international company with its footprint all over the globe. In the United States, it has customers in the food-processing industry that include baked goods companies like General Mills, Inc., McKee Foods Corporation, and Sara Lee Corporation. Its Brazilian food-processing customers include Nestle, Groupe Danone, and Nabisco.

It also has food-service customers in the United States, including Sysco Corporation; Ruby Tuesday, Inc.; Krispy Kreme Doughnuts, Inc.; and Yum! Brands, Inc. And even in Brazil, Bunge is a major supplier of frying and baking shortening to McDonald's Corporation. It has European clients like Unilever and Nestle.

Any time you buy a stock, you take a risk. But if you're looking for a strong stock to capitalize on a fundamental economic demand—food, both the growing of it and the processing and selling of it—Bunge is the ticket.

Action to Take

Buy shares of **Bunge** (NYSE: BG) at market. As always, use a 25 percent trailing stop

to protect your profits and your capital. (See pages 26–28 for trailing stop information.) Please note: Visit www.investmentu.com /china for important updates regarding this specific recommendation.

Opportunity 3: These 25 Hot China Stocks Can Lower Your Portfolio Risk

Here is a way to invest in China growth and still sleep at night. It's a simple plan to capture the upside while minimizing risk if the Chinese economy hits a speed bump.

Launched in October 2004, the **iShares FTSE/Xinhua China 25 Index Fund** (FXI) is comprised of 25 of the largest and most liquid China names. All of the 25 stocks included in the China iShare are listed on the Hong Kong Stock Exchange. Some of them are incorporated in mainland China (H shares) and some of them are incorporated in Hong Kong (red chips). The China iShare has been picking up steam in the last few months and is up 25.58 percent nine months into 2006.

This ETF provides good exposure to three key sectors of China: energy (20 percent), telecom (19 percent), and industrial (18 percent). The top five companies represent 40 percent of the index. The annual operating expenses of the China iShare are only 0.74 percent compared to 2 percent plus for other alternatives out there including actively managed China and greater China regional funds. Keep in mind that most of these companies are still largely controlled and owned by the Chinese government.

Since indexing outpaces the majority of active mutual fund products accompanied by low fees, the FXI offers the best exposure to Mainland China stocks.

The fund currently charges 0.74 percent per annum in expenses, and manages $892 million in assets. Trading volume on the New York Stock Exchange for FXI is also very liquid.

Some of the largest constituents in the FTSE/Xinhua China 25 Index Fund are China Mobile, PetroChina Company, BOC Hong Kong, China Petroleum and Chemical Corporation (Sinopec), and China Life Insurance Company, the world's largest initial public offering in 2005.

With chunks of China Petroleum and PetroChina, FXI is a great diversified way to profit from the huge demand and dwindling supplies of oil. Like we said earlier, oil consumption by China has more than doubled in the past decade and it is expected to grow by 7.4 percent this year, from last year's blistering 16 percent rate.

Even the newest discovery of oil in the Gulf of Mexico won't be ready for production until approximately 2010 or so. Even then, analysts say it isn't going to make a dent in reserves or the ongoing growing demand.

New Bankruptcy Law Bodes Well for Banks

The three largest publicly traded Chinese banks (Bank of China, China Construction Bank, and Bank of Communications) are not listed in the United States. However, each of them is part of FXI for a combined 15 percent of assets. Because China now has its first formal corporate-bankruptcy process after the Enterprise Bankruptcy Law following 12 years of deliberation, this trio of banks stands to benefit.

China's creditor banks stand to benefit most. However, given already high valuations, new buying induced by the bankruptcy law is unlikely but is at least seen as supporting current valuations.

Three of China's five largest banks trade publicly with valuations ranging from 16 to 21 times expected earnings, compared to Hong-Kong listed banks averaging 15 times and U.S. banks at 12 times. The current delinquent loan recovery rate in China is near 30 percent for the most recently issued loans and it is expected to approach to the global average of 70 percent via the newly enacted bankruptcy law.

The road to rehabilitation for China's capital markets won't be easy, and will certainly be accompanied by incredible volatility; but that's exactly what we expect from this country, home to one of the world's cheapest markets following a series of crashes.

Playing China directly through an index fund is probably one of the best investment decisions for 2006/2007 should the market decline.

Action to Take

Buy the **iShares FTSE/Xinhua China 25 Index Fund** (NYSE-FXI) at market. Use a 25 percent trailing stop to protect profits and principal. (See pages 26–28 for trailing stop information.) Please note: Visit www.investmentu .com/china for important updates regarding this specific recommendation.

Opportunity 4: How a Conservative Bank in London Could Be the Best China Play of All

It's not news that many respected analysts predict that China, and shortly thereafter, India, will be the world's main economic superpowers within a relatively few short years. Investing in China presents some challenges (and requires a deft touch). For instance, the banking sector in China is particularly attractive.

For years, hundreds of millions of middle-class Chinese had the desire for modern goods and services. Now, they finally have the means. And demand for checking and savings accounts, credit cards, commercial and home loans, financial planning, and investment banking services is soaring.

Behind this roaring demand for financial services, though, lies a banking sector in considerable disrepair. In fact, according to Goldman Sachs, nonperforming loans now account for an unthinkable 50 percent of China's output. And with financial transparency practically nonexistent in China, it's especially hard to sort out the good banks from the bad.

Luckily, there's a way to invest and capture the soaring demand for China's banking services, without taking on the high risk associated with the Shanghai Stock Market.

Our Best "China Play" Just May Be a British Bank . . .

Allow us to explain. . . .

One of the basics of emerging markets investing is to know the local dynamics that drive these exotic economies. Just ask Chicago-based Motorola. The company squandered roughly $1.8 billion in Turkey because it failed to find out exactly how this emerging economy worked before making an investment.

When it comes to China, though, a little gumption and in-country homework wouldn't be enough to save us from the same fate as Motorola. The reason: China's capital markets are just too darned young.

In fact, the Chinese stock market is only 15 years old. And that's hardly enough time to understand the dynamics of an economy 1.3 billion consumers strong, or to extract any meaningful patterns from the data to determine undervalued and overlooked stocks.

So instead of letting your money ride in China on a whim and a prayer, it's best to go with a company with a bit more experience . . . and a proven track record. With over 100 years of experience investing in China, one company also has a 10-year track record that includes:

- Total operating income growth of 15.8 percent
- Operating profit increases of 18.1 percent
- Earnings per share growth of 11.8 percent
- And a hefty dividend per share growth of 16.8 percent

We'd be hard pressed to find a better China play, even if the company is headquartered in London.

HSBC Is Way Ahead of the Pack. Understanding the enormous influence that China is about to exert on the world economy is crucial to understanding the superb business prospects of HSBC Holdings.

For instance, according to Andy Xie, an economist with Morgan Stanley in Hong Kong, "China's rise as a manufacturing base is going to have the same kind of impact on the world that the industrialization of the United States had, perhaps even bigger."

HSBC, however, is already way ahead of them. With operations in virtually every business district throughout Asia, this $105 billion bank is going to be a prime beneficiary of the explosive impact that China is about to have on the world economy.

This Company's Financial Position Is a Fortress

The company we're referring to is HSBC (NYSE:HBC). Headquartered in London, HSBC—originally known as the Hongkong and Shanghai Banking Corporation—is the world's third-largest bank. And its self-branded tag line as the "World's Local Bank" speaks volumes.

Since its meager beginnings in Hong Kong in 1865, the company now operates more than 9,800 offices in 77 countries across the globe. And it's still growing. But why is HSBC a relatively safe way to invest in China? For two simple reasons: There's no other company that can lay claim to courting and keeping Chinese customers for more than 100 years; and no other company has a stronger foothold in China.

On top of its own operations and branches that span the country, HSBC also owns strategic stakes in four extremely promising Chinese companies: Bank of Communications (19.9 percent), Ping An (19.9 percent), Industrial Bank of China (15.98 percent), and Bank of Shanghai (8 percent). If it weren't for government regulations restricting foreign firms from holding more than a 19.9 percent stake in a Chinese company, we're certain HSBC would have probably acquired a few of the companies outright.

Much More Than Just a China Play

Through its partnerships and its own business experience that spans over 100 years, you'd be hard pressed to find another company better equipped to understand and profit from China's torrid growth.

But HSBC is much more than just a China play. The company is also expanding into emerging economies, offering similar profit potential. It's estimated that 50 percent of the increase in world demand will come from the developing countries of China, India, Mexico, and Brazil. We know HSBC has China covered. But it turns out it's on top of the other opportunities, as well.

In Mexico, the company boasts a 33 percent market share in ATMs, and most recently doubled its market share of remittances (money sent from one place or person to another).

In Brazil, the company boasts a database of more than 25 million customers, and pretax profits soared over 200 percent last year. And HSBC has expanded quickly in India. Not to mention that pretax profits more than doubled last year in the rest of the Asia Pacific.

Expect Double-Digit Growth from This "Uncommonly Safe Investment"

HSBC's appeal goes well beyond its strategic and unparalleled growth opportunities. Above all, HSBC is an uncommonly safe investment. Here's why: Earnings are well balanced geographically and by customer group. Such diversity makes it near impossible for a single event to shatter this company's strong foundation. In fact, despite the company's exposure to the Argentina crisis in 2001, revenues that year barely flinched.

And given the company's breadth of operations and expansion, expect revenues to grow at a steady double-digit pace well into the future.

On top of that, HSBC's various business segments provide a diversity of revenue streams, proven to rake in consistent revenues and profits throughout the twists and turns of every business cycle.

And perhaps most impressive is management's frugality. Unlike other traditional banks that spend mindlessly and offer countless perks, executives at HSBC operate much differently: They try to maximize shareholder value in every single action.

Even the Chairman Flies Coach

At HSBC, you won't find exorbitant salaries— and company stock options are conservatively granted. The chairman even refuses to fly anything but coach class.

This conservatism also enters management's decision-making process. Known for its countless acquisitions, HSBC refuses to buy a firm unless the deal adds to earnings in the first year.

In summary, the company's frugal habits ensure we get much more value than we could have bargained for. Especially since shares trade at a trailing 12-month price/earnings ratio of 14.05 (for comparison, the ratio for HSBC's peer group and the S&P 500 are roughly 19.5).

HSBC represents an impressive alternative to investing inside China itself. And with its global growth opportunities, diversity of revenue streams, frugal management, hefty profit margins, and relationships with over 70 percent of the *Fortune* 500, it's an opportunity that will last much longer than the China craze. And it even pays a nice 4 percent dividend yield.

Action to Take

Buy **HSBC** (NYSE: HBC) or, if you already own it, add to your position. And use our regular 25 percent trailing stop to protect profits and principal. (See pages 26–28 for trailing stop information.) Please note: Visit www.investmentu.com /china for important updates regarding this specific recommendation.

Our Secret to Success: The Investment U Philosophy

Our philosophy of investing is this: You can't go too far wrong if you get the big questions right. The big questions are not, "when will the economy recover?" or, "where will the market go next?"

True, these are the questions that most investors obsess over. But it's a waste of your time. The big questions—the important ones that you can take action on—are these:

1. How can I get the highest return with the least amount of risk?
2. How can I protect both profits and principal?
3. What can I do to GUARANTEE my investment portfolio will be worth more in the future?

Here are three fundamental and key parts of the Investment U philosophy—a trailing stop strategy, asset allocation, and position sizing—and how together they can make this year, and your future ones, very prosperous.

Limit Your Downside by Using a "Trailing Stop Strategy"

At Investment U, we always look for the best and brightest stars to grow your portfolio, and we employ a secret weapon that is proven to get you the lion's share of any move.

When you buy a stock, you buy it with the intention to sell it for a profit some time in the future.

In order to do so successfully, you should put as much thought into planning your exit strategy as you put into the research that motivates you to buy the investment in the first place.

Becoming a Top Trader ... Psychologically Speaking. Investment U Advisory Panel member Dr. Van K. Tharp is "coach" to the world's greatest investors and traders. These superstars come to Dr. Tharp (he has a three-month waiting list according to **USA Today**) for stock market investment advice that will lift their profits to even higher levels.

During the past 20 years, Dr. Tharp has accumulated psychological profiles on over 4,000 investors from all around the globe. To maintain current profile data, he has conducted many follow-up interviews with them. In addition, he has conducted extensive, in-person interviews with many of the world's best investors and traders.

Two techniques were used by a full 99 percent of these investors. In other words, they disagreed on almost everything else—but a full 99 percent believed that these two techniques were essential to their success.

One, of course, was to never ever lose big money in the stock market (a.k.a. using a trailing stop loss).

To find out the other, visit http://www.investmentu.com/resources/investmentadvice.html.

Our advice is to follow this simple plan: We ride our stocks as high as we can, but if they head for a crash, we have our exit strategy in place to protect us from damage. Though we have many levels of defense and many reasons we could sell a stock, if our reasons don't appear before the crash, the Trailing Stop Strategy is our last-ditch measure to save our hard-earned dollars. And, as you'll see, it works well.

The main element to Investment U's trailing stop strategy is a 25 percent rule. We will sell positions at 25 percent off their highs. For example, if we buy a stock at $50, and it rises to $100, when do we sell it? When it falls back to $75, or 25 percent off our high.

If you limit your losses to 25 percent per investment, you at least have a fighting chance of getting that money back. If you allow larger drops, you're going to be a loser over the long run. No doubt about it.

If you do hold onto a falling stock too long, the loss will often be far more than just 25 percent. And all it takes is one big loss to set an investor back for years.

Let's say you start off with $10,000. A year later you've made 25 percent ($12,500). Same for next year ($15,625), and the next ($19,530). But then after three years of 25 percent annual gains, the fourth year, you take a loss of 50 percent. It puts you back below where you started, at $9,766.

Now, let's say you had a 25 percent trailing stop during the year you lost 50 percent. You would have been stopped out at $14,648. Then during the following three years (when you again profited by 25 percent each year), your holdings would be $28,600 at the end of that entire seven-year stretch.

However, if you didn't have a 25 percent trailing stop in place, after the same seven-year period, you would only have $19,073, still below where you were prior to the 50 percent drop.

Over the seven years of this example, you'd be up 186 percent. That's an average return of over 26 percent per year, much better than you'd think. But pick your own example, and do the math. Look back at your own portfolio. You'll see that cutting your losses is the key to both getting good overall returns and avoiding lost years.

This is best illustrated by some specific examples—real recommendations made by Investment U And fortunately, the tech run-up and subsequent meltdown provided substantial proof that limiting your downside gives you more capital to invest in your winners.

Let's begin with a look at Adobe, the innovative software company on the (then) booming Nasdaq. It zoomed up, with no sizable price correction, for 10 straight months. The stock kept achieving new all-time highs. Along the way, we would have kept adjusting upward our 25 percent trailing stop. Given that we would have bought in at $31, we would have kept locking in higher and higher profits.

When the technology and communications sectors finally began to correct, Adobe corrected along with them. But thanks to our 25 percent trailing stop, the worst-case result for our investment would have been a profit of over 81 percent (down 25 percent from it's highest price).

Several companies witnessed declines of as much as 90 percent, and the "buy-and-hold" crowd held all the way down. That's what can happen when you hold a stock investment with no exit strategy. That kind of loss is hard to recover from.

In reality, most investors who say they're buying and holding will in fact panic in a bear market, especially a long grinding one. We saw it graphically in 2000 to 2002—the last bear market. Don't let this happen to you: Use a smart exit strategy that lets you capture the majority of any profits—even a doomed one.

Position Sizing Is What the Pros Do That Novices Don't

For the world's most successful investors, low risk means entering only into positions where the probability for high profits far exceeds the possibility of losses over the long run. They invest their money in such a way as to position themselves for maximum profits while—at the very same time—ensuring that their exposure to serious loss is absolutely nonexistent.

Position sizing is really all about money management. But it's not the kind you use to make sure you have enough money on hand to pay expenses like the mortgage, household bills, college tuition for your children, car payments, and so on.

The money management connected with position sizing is strictly limited to your investment portfolio. And it's every bit as crucial to your profits as trailing stops and the stocks you choose.

That's because this management process tells you how much you should invest in your positions so that you're not risking more than you're comfortable with. Position sizing also helps you when you decide it's time to add to your winning investments—a process we'll discuss in a moment.

Investment Advice in the Form of a Marble Game

At many of his seminars, Dr. Tharp illustrates the importance of position sizing by having the participants play an investment game using a bag of marbles. At the start of the marble game, participants are each given $100,000 in play money to seed their portfolio. There are 20 marbles in the bag, each one representing either a losing (black marble) or a winning (white marble) trade. There's one more interesting variable: 60 percent of the marbles in the bag are winners while 40 percent are losers. And each marble is replaced after it is drawn.

One of the winners is a "10 times winner," and one of the losers is a "5 times loser." The odds of winning in this marble game are far higher than the odds we face in the markets. Still, when Dr. Tharp conducts this game with his seminar audiences, more than two-thirds of the participants always lose money. And a full one-third goes bankrupt.

How is that possible? How can a majority of people lose in a game in which the odds are so heavily in their favor?

The answer is very simple: Those who lose money do so because they have no idea how much they should be investing in any one marble draw. They are playing the game without a "system," so they're really doing nothing but gambling. This sort of approach doesn't win the marble game. And, in the real-world investment game, it won't lead to long-term wealth.

The key to success they're missing in the marble game—and the strategy you should use in your portfolio—is position sizing.

Successful Investing Is Emotionless Investing

Just as we saw when we were looking at trailing stops, investors in this marble game lose money because they get caught up in the emotions of investing. During his marble game, Dr. Tharp does just what's needed to push all the "hot buttons" of his audience. . . .

For example, after 10 pulls from the bag, he'll ask to see the hands of all those whose play-money portfolios have doubled in value. And a few hands always go up. Of course, when the others in the game—the vast majority—see that a few of their fellow participants have hit it big already, worry and envy enter the picture. And what do you think happens?

In an attempt to catch up with the winners, the other participants start increasing their bets. Problem is, when these ill-considered bets turn out to be losers, they're doomed to failure—they dig themselves into a hole they can't get out of.

Now, we'll show you how you could win in this marble game. It's the same way you'll win in the real-life investing game—the game that will determine the level of wealth you're going to attain in this life. Here's how you can pursue the very same low-risk ideas the world's best investors go after.

First of all, we're assuming that you'll be following our investment advice and always have 25 percent trailing stops on your investments. The 25 percent is our rule—you can choose your own percentage. The most important thing is that you use it consistently.

Based on this assumption, for your investments to be low-risk, you should be dealing with odds of at least *2-to-1* or *3-to-1* in your favor, and that means you should be expecting returns of between 50 percent and 75 percent on your profitable investments.

We arrive at those figures knowing that because you'll never lose more than 25 percent on any one investment (you'll be stopped out at a 25 percent loss), 50 percent and 75 percent gains represent, respectively, 2-to-1 and 3-to-1 odds.

To give you another example, let's say you invest in a stock that you expect to return only 30 percent rather than 50 percent or 75 percent. To keep your investment low risk (and your odds at 3-to-1), you'd have to change your trailing stop from 25 percent to 10 percent. Whatever your expected profits, here are two "golden rules" you should follow:

1. Know your worst-case scenario to keep from going bankrupt.
2. Determine how much you're willing to lose in any one investment.

Now we'll see how you would apply these two golden rules to Dr. Tharp's marble game in order to come out a winner.

You'd first have to decide how much of your $100,000 you were willing to lose on any one marble pull. Now, because you're adhering to Investment U's 25 percent trailing stop rule that decision won't be difficult for you—you know that 25 percent is the *maximum* you're ever going to lose. So you would never want to put more than 5 percent of your money on any one marble—because if you were to pull that 5 times loser out of the bag, you'd hit your stop-loss limit (5 percent × 5 percent = 25 percent).

You'd have to start with a bet of $5,000 (5 percent of $100,000). But what would you do next? Would you simply continue to bet $5,000 on every marble you pulled from the bag? Well, because the odds of this game are heavily stacked in your favor, that strategy would probably mean you'd end the game with more money than when you started.

So it would be a good strategy—but it's not the best you can do. To really optimize the profit on your investments—in the marble game or in real life—you should scale the size of your investments to the amount of total capital you have in your portfolio.

Always Know Exactly How Much to Invest in the Market for Maximum Profit and Comfort

If in the marble game your portfolio had grown from the starting $100,000 to $200,000, and you want to stick with your 5 percent rule, then instead of investing $5,000 on your next investment, you'd go with $10,000. Your risk stays the same (a $10,000 investment in a $200,000 portfolio is the same as a $5,000 investment in a $100,000 portfolio), but your potential for profit escalates because you have more money in play. Similarly, if you happen to start out with some losses, you only risk 5 percent of what remains in your portfolio.

For your initial investment and for all subsequent investments, you should never take on a bigger risk than you're comfortable with. And you should have a systematic way of investing that ensures that no matter how the size of your portfolio changes, you'll continue to maintain that same risk level.

The advice we give at Investment U. includes a strong recommendation that you never have more than 2 percent of your capital at risk in any one position. But remember, that doesn't mean that you can only invest 2 percent in any one position—it means you shouldn't have more than 2 percent at risk.

To illustrate this 2 percent rule, let's look at a $100,000 portfolio. If you follow our rule for 25 percent trailing stops and 2 percent risk, the maximum you can invest in any one stock at any one time is $8,000. Here's the formula for figuring that out: $[(0.02 \times 100,000)/0.25]$. Now here it is "spelled out": 0.02 times 100,000 = 2,000, divided by 0.25 = 8,000.

If you decided you wanted to put less at risk—1 percent of your capital—our formula would be $[(0.01 \times 100,000)/0.25])$ and your limit would be $4,000 in any one stock.

The central message here is consistency: Decide on how much you want to risk, and then stick with that number no matter what. Stay with low-risk ideas, have a consistent exit strategy for the stock market, and you'll begin to make money just like the world's greatest investors.

Stick to an Asset Allocation Model

Successful investing begins by conceding that—to a degree—uncertainty will always be your companion. You can guess what the market is going to do and be right or you can guess and be wrong. Or you can let some self-styled "expert" do the guessing for you. But no one guesses right consistently, so we don't waste time here.

Instead, we follow an investment formula that won Dr. Harold Markowitz the Nobel Prize in finance in 1990. His paper promising "portfolio optimization through means variance analysis" demonstrates how you can maximize your profits and minimize your risk by properly asset allocating and rebalancing your portfolio.

As far as nuts and bolts, the first step in asset allocation is dividing your portfolio into baskets, or asset classes. In today's investment landscape, there are a multitude of them. They include: stocks, bonds, cash (not simply cash in your wallet or bank, but also highly liquid and secure short-term instruments such as T-Bills, money market funds and CDs) real estate and precious metals.

Subclasses exist within these major asset classes. For instance, stocks aren't exclusive to the Dow, S&P 500 and Nasdaq. Rather, stock classes range from large-caps, mid-caps, and small-caps, to growth stocks, value stocks, or emerging market stocks.

Diversification and Correlation . . . Limiting Assets That Behave the Same

Diversification is a strategy that reduces portfolio volatility and exposure to risk by combining a variety of investments that are unlikely to move in the same direction in the same conditions. In other words, the asset classes in your portfolio should not be correlated.

Instead, you want to take advantage of the fact that unrelated investments will behave differently at any given point in time. For instance, in 2005 while large-cap stocks (represented by the Dow Jones Industrial Average) returned – 0.61 percent, real estate investment trusts (REITs) (represented by the Dow Jones Equity REIT Total Return Index) rose 11.9 percent.

A simple and good way to accomplish this is by owning stocks and bonds. An even better one is to use mutual funds because they are already diversified by virtue of owning sometimes hundreds of stocks in one fund. When you mix up your portfolio with funds among different asset classes, the chance that more than one will drop at the same time diminishes further.

Odds are also very low that two or more mutual funds will hold the same stocks. And, if you use a no-load commission-free family or discount brokerage, mutual funds can be very cost-effective.

Ultimately, diversification reduces the upside and downside potential of your portfolio. As a result, you are protected against wild fluctuations and volatility, something most investors wish they had when global tensions mount or when the markets sell off, sometimes for no good reason.

Asset allocation actually takes diversification and correlation a step further by considering the varying risks associated with each asset class. For example, stocks have produced historically higher-than-average annual returns and more volatility than other investments.

Bonds, on the other hand, perform steadily over time. They may generate lower returns than stocks, but their prices fluctuate far less.

Harry Markowitz's strategy calls for a melting pot of investments for your portfolio, mixing high- and low-risk assets to create the perfect blend of risk versus reward for you, personally.

For instance, a young aggressive investor wants and needs capital appreciation for growth. This person's allocation might be 70 percent to 80 percent in stocks and the rest in bonds and/ or cash.

As this investor ages and looks to preserve wealth and reduce risk, he will need more dividend-producing holdings to generate income from his assets. It's an easy shift: Allocate less to the riskier asset class of stocks and more to the lower risk classes of bonds and cash. The portfolio might have 80 percent in bonds and 20 percent in stocks or 0 percent in stocks and 20 percent in cash.

Despite these guidelines, you are the only one who knows how much risk lets you sleep at night. Can you handle a 35 percent loss in a year or would you rather see a conservative growth rate of 10 percent and not be subject to higher losses?

All we can do is arm you with the facts. Only you know how much risk you can stomach. Here are some historical rewards versus risk numbers:

- Safe portfolio—20 percent stocks, 80 percent bonds:
  - —Throughout history, this portfolio has averaged 7.0 percent a year.
  - —Its WORST year was a loss of 10.1 percent.
  - —It lost money 17 percent of the years.
- Balanced portfolio—50 percent stocks, 50 percent bonds
  - —Throughout history, this portfolio has averaged 8.7 percent a year.
  - —Its WORST year was a loss of 22.5 percent.
  - —It lost money 22 percent of the years.
- Risky portfolio—80 percent stocks, 20 percent bonds
  - —Throughout history, this portfolio has averaged 10.0 percent a year.
  - —Its WORST year was a loss of 34.9 percent.
  - —It lost money 28 percent of the years.

The Rebalancing Act: "Buy and Hold" Is Not an Investment Strategy

After using asset allocation to divide investments across different asset classes, there is one more critical component to understand—it's the 15 minutes of work you'll have to do annually, and it's known as "rebalancing."

Many investors did well during the roaring bull market of the 1990s. But the thundering herd turned into cliff-diving lemmings when the market downdraft started in earnest six years ago.

Why didn't these investors sell? In many cases, it was because their money managers or mutual fund companies peddled the idea that you should buy and sit tight. Not a bad marketing idea if you run a mutual fund company with millions of dollars in management fees and other expenses rolling in annually from shareholders.

But let's face facts. Any successful investment strategy includes a sell discipline. Otherwise, you're just acting on blind faith. Faith that often turns out to be unjustified.

But the decision to sell is complicated because history has shown that it is impossible to predict which asset class will be the best or the worst in any given year.

If you look specifically at 1999, Long-Term Government Bonds were the worst performing asset class of the group at −9.0 percent. The very next year, though, they led all asset classes with returns of 21.5 percent.

Or take the example of Small-Cap Stocks. In 2002, they posted negative returns (−13.3 percent). In 2003, they rose to the top, up 45.4 percent.

Since no one can predict the market leaders and underperformers, you must stay in the market over time to reach your financial goals. And you must remain allocated across a broad group of asset classes. That's why a proper asset allocation also involves the strategy of rebalancing.

Rebalancing is a tool to help you maintain your target allocation by selling a portion of an appreciated asset and investing the proceeds into an underweighted asset class to restore your original asset allocation.

To understand this, consider that the following asset classes—stocks, bonds, precious metals, and so on—represent a specific percentage of your total portfolio.

But as each year goes by, those percentages change depending on the performance of the financial markets. Bonds may be higher, and stocks may be lower.

Inflation-adjusted Treasuries may have appreciated, and gold mining shares may have fallen. And so on. The job of rebalancing is to bring those percentages back to your original alignment.

Let's walk through an example to show you the ease and importance of rebalancing. For this example, let's use an asset allocation that is 30 percent U.S. stocks, 10 percent international stocks, 50 percent U.S. bonds, and 10 percent cash.

Let's assume at the end of the year the portfolio value is $140,000. U.S. stocks performed strongly, international stocks struggled, and U.S. bonds and cash were relatively stable.

To rebalance this portfolio, $7,000 of U.S. stocks and $2,800 of U.S. bonds would have to be sold to reallocate $9,800 to international stocks, thereby returning the portfolio to its original asset allocation percentages.

Instead of ascribing to the "buy-and-hold" philosophy, asset allocation forces you to sell investments on an annual basis. Logic might tell you to sell your worst-performers. Not so. You actually sell the top-performers and reallocate to the lowest performers.

It doesn't just hope to "buy low and sell high." It forces you to actually do it. If you didn't rebalance, you would be buying more of an appreciated asset in the hope that you will be able to sell it at an even higher price in the future.

Remember that it is impossible to predict which asset class will be the best- or worst-performing in any given year. So although international stocks may have underperformed in the previous year, there is no way of being certain that they won't be one of the top performers the following year.

Rebalancing your portfolio ensures your investments are always properly allocated to take advantage of these year-to-year changes.

When markets are performing poorly, your rebalanced portfolio will experience less negative returns than a "nonrebalanced" portfolio, which translates into greater portfolio value during such times. And when the markets turn, you'll have more money to take advantage of the upswing than you would if you didn't rebalance.

Author Biographies

Alexander Green is investment director of *The Oxford Club*. A Wall Street veteran, he has more than 20 years' experience as a research analyst, investment advisor, and professional portfolio manager.

Mr. Green has been featured on *The O'Reilly Factor*, profiled by *Forbes* and Marketwatch .com, and has written for Louis Rukeyser and several other leading financial publishers.

He currently writes and directs *The Oxford Club's Communiqué*, the *Oxford Insight* and *More Green Stuff* e-letters, and three elite trading services: *The Momentum Alert*, *The Insider Alert* and *The International Trader Alert*. He also co-edits *The Oxford Short Alert* with Louis Bass. Alex is a top-rated speaker at financial conferences throughout the world.

Horacio Márquez is editor of the *Money Map Advantage*, and has more than 20 years of experience in global finance activities on Wall Street, in major U.S. fund management companies and independently.

Mr. Márquez was head of Emerging Markets Research for Merrill Lynch Asset Management's Fixed-Income Funds; director and head of Economic and Financial Research—Latin America for Swiss Bank and head of Credit and Research for ADP Capital Management. In these capacities, while managing billions of dollars, he correctly foresaw and took advantage of the Argentine fiscal crisis of 1994, the Mexican maxi-devaluation later that year, the Asian crisis of 1997, and the Russian crisis of 1998.

He got out of Enron, WorldCom, and many other stocks without losses well before they defaulted and foresaw the ensuing U.S. recession and recovery. Mr. Márquez has also worked independently in M&A, venture capital, and debt financing in Latin America and in the United States. He holds an MS in Industrial Administration from Carnegie-Mellon's Tepper Business School.

Louis Bass is the editor of the *Hot IPO Trader*, an alert service uncovering the hottest and most potentially profitable IPOs. He's also the editor of the *Takeover Trader* alert service, targeting takeover candidates poised for triple-digit gains.

As an advisory panelist for *The Oxford Club,* Mr. Bass is also the co-editor of the *Oxford Hedge Trader* and is a regular contributor to the *Club*'s twice-monthly *Communiqué*.

Mr. Bass spent years with one of the country's leading investment and brokerage firms as a top analyst and trading expert, specializing in corporate takeovers and IPOs that led to large profit opportunities for investors.

Mark Whistler writes and conducts research for *The Oxford Club* and *Mt. Vernon Research* and is the author of the recently released book *Trading Pairs* (John Wiley & Sons, Inc., 2004), and is one of two creators of PairsTrader.com.

Mr. Whistler is presently working on his second book on market psychology for Wiley, expected to be on shelves toward the end of 2006.

He writes a regular column for Traderdaily.com in New York and also writes for Investopedia.com in Canada, for whom he recently finished a Series 63 study guide. A few of his other writing credentials include: *The Motley Fool, Active Trader Magazine,* BullMarket.com, OptionInvestor.com, and *Working-Money Online*.

Here's How to Get Updates on Every Recommendation in This Report . . .

The companies in this report offer tremendous upside. And while their outlook is favorable for the long run, it's critical you have access to up-to-the-minute, material information regarding these recommendations.

We've set up a web site that gives you current information and will report any significant developments. It is exclusive to those who have purchased this report.

Visit www.investmentu.com/china to confirm your purchase, and we will immediately deliver the company updates via e-mail.

Your confirmation will also provide you with unlimited and free access to all of Investment U's current market research—26 investor reports, including:

√ A "New" Stock Play on Alternative Energy—Why Now Is the Time to Invest in Ethanol

√ Knowing When Stocks Are Set to Soar—How to Uncover Momentum Plays

That Can Turn $10,000 into $1 Million or More

√ Unearthing Profitable Opportunities in the Red-Hot Copper Market

In addition, through the *Investment U E-Letter*, you'll also get current market coverage from Dr. Mark Skousen, chairman of Investment U, author of more than 20 financial books and former columnist for *Forbes* magazine.

Your express access includes U.S. and foreign stock market advice, precious metals reports, how to invest in overseas real estate markets . . . even how to invest in gold coins. In all, there are more than 500 articles.

Investment U:
What No Books, No Schools,
No Brokers Will Teach You
www.investmentu.com